B1

THINK-A-GRAMS

EVELYNE M. GRAHAM

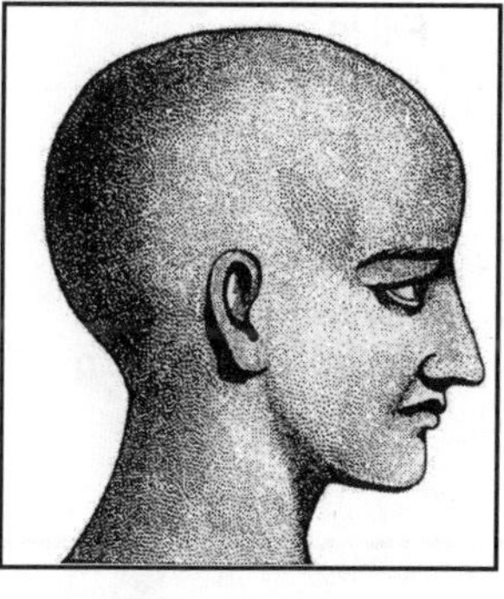

THE CRITICAL THINKING CO.
(BRIGHT MINDS™)
www.CriticalThinking.com
P.O. Box 1610 • Seaside • CA 93955-1610
Phone 800-458-4849 • FAX 831-393-3277
ISBN 0-89455-330-5

Printed in the United States of America

TEACHER SUGGESTIONS AND ANSWERS

SUGGESTIONS

THINK-A-GRAMS are verbal picture puzzlers. They can be posted individually, either daily or weekly, on a bulletin board to sharpen students' thinking.

In terms of difficulty, the A level is easiest, B more difficult, and the C level is hardest. Within levels, books 1 and 2 are of similar difficulty.

Each of the books in this series contains an answer key and 100 page-size puzzles. The puzzles provide teachers with an entertaining and challenging tool for coordinating right-brain thinking with left-brain memory. To solve these puzzles, the right brain analyzes the puzzle's symbology and the left brain recalls the common term or phrase depicted.

Since schools devote so much curricula to such left-brain activities as memorization and regurgitation, exposure to more right-brain experiences, such as these THINK-A-GRAMS, helps students develop skills in spatial relations, creative thinking, and problem solving.

Keep in mind that there is frequently more than one answer to a given problem. Encourage students to invent their own THINK-A-GRAMS for your classroom!

ABOUT THE AUTHOR

EVELYNE GRAHAM has 34 years of teaching experience—including all 12 grades—with a major discipline in mathematics. She spent 20 years as Supervisor of Mathematics for Chesapeake Public School System (Virginia), 6 years as Assistant Principal of Instruction at Chesapeake Alternative School, and 10 years as an extension instructor in Mathematics for Elementary Teachers for the University of Virginia.

Mrs. Graham holds an undergraduate degree with triple majors in math, religious education, and music, a masters degree in Mathematics Education, and a Certificate of Advanced Study in School Administration.

Mrs. Graham is a frequent presenter at state and national conferences and the author of books and articles about mathematics education and activities.

ANSWERS B1

1. Cutting back
2. Change of heart
3. Walk on by
4. Weekend vacation
5. Amended bylaws
6. Come forth
7. Three strikes-you're out
8. Racial bigotry
9. Low tide
10. Two left feet
11. Pretty please with sugar on it
12. Fun under the sun
13. Tumult
14. Strong overtones
15. Peak performance
16. Up until now
17. Green overcoat
18. Beating around the bush
19. Two peas in a pod
20. Hands-on activities
21. Caught in the middle
22. First-class mail
23. Heaven on earth
24. Fun and games
25. For instance
26. Splitting headache
27. Down to earth
28. Up for grabs
29. Neon sign
30. Try in vain
31. Topic under discussion
32. Arm in arm
33. Highfalutin
34. Feedback
35. Back to square one
36. It's about time
37. Too funny for words
38. Cracking up
39. All across the nation
40. Talking back
41. Time on my hands
42. Truth-in-lending
43. Four score and seven
44. First pair
45. Highway overpass
46. Cover up
47. Order in advance
48. Center of attention
49. Bottomless pit
50. Walking on cloud nine
51. Lost in the crowd
52. Chasing after girls
53. Walking through the yellow pages
54. Dressed to kill
55. In over my head
56. Sidewinder
57. Tuna fish
58. Side effect
59. A play on words
60. War between nations
61. A song in the air
62. Worked overtime
63. Real lowdown
64. A crack in the ice
65. Head-on collision
66. Top dollar
67. Learn by rote
68. Power in high places
69. Up the creek
70. Painless operations
71. Sailing on the seven seas
72. Hand in glove
73. Swim underwater
74. Call before you come
75. Sunday overalls
76. An inside job
77. Rambling around
78. Fall back
79. Friendly undertaker
80. Hygiene
81. A ban on smoking
82. Car overhauled
83. Down yonder
84. Goose down
85. Strong undertow
86. Caught in the act
87. Pipe down
88. Ride in comfort
89. Getting through the day
90. Down on his luck
91. Brood over mistakes
92. Give up in despair
93. Fill 'er up
94. April in Paris
95. Trial by error
96. Read all about it
97. I give up
98. A chat over lunch
99. Inside information
100. Realignment

THINK-A-GRAM B1

THINK-A-GRAM B1

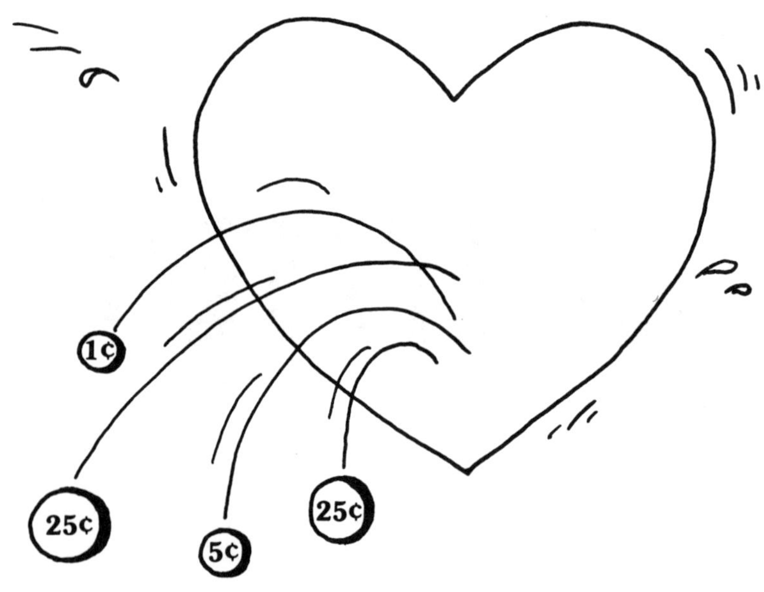

THINK-A-GRAM B1

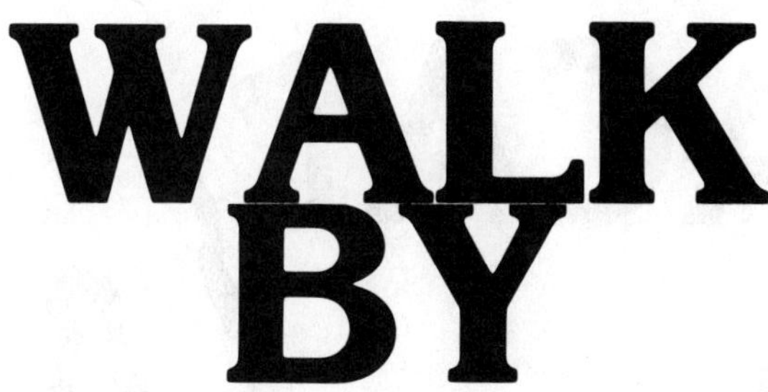

THINK-A-GRAM B1

AMENDED LAWS

THINK-A-GRAM B1

~~COME~~
~~COME~~
~~COME~~
COME

THINK-A-GRAM B1

STRIKE STRIKE STRIKE	YOUR

RACIAL

OTRY

THINK-A-GRAM B1

THINK-A-GRAM B1

LEFT FEET
LEFT FEET

THINK-A-GRAM B1

SUN

FUN

THINK-A-GRAM B1

STRONG

TONES

THINK-A-GRAM B1

THINK-A-GRAM B1

GREEN
COAT

THINK-A-GRAM B1

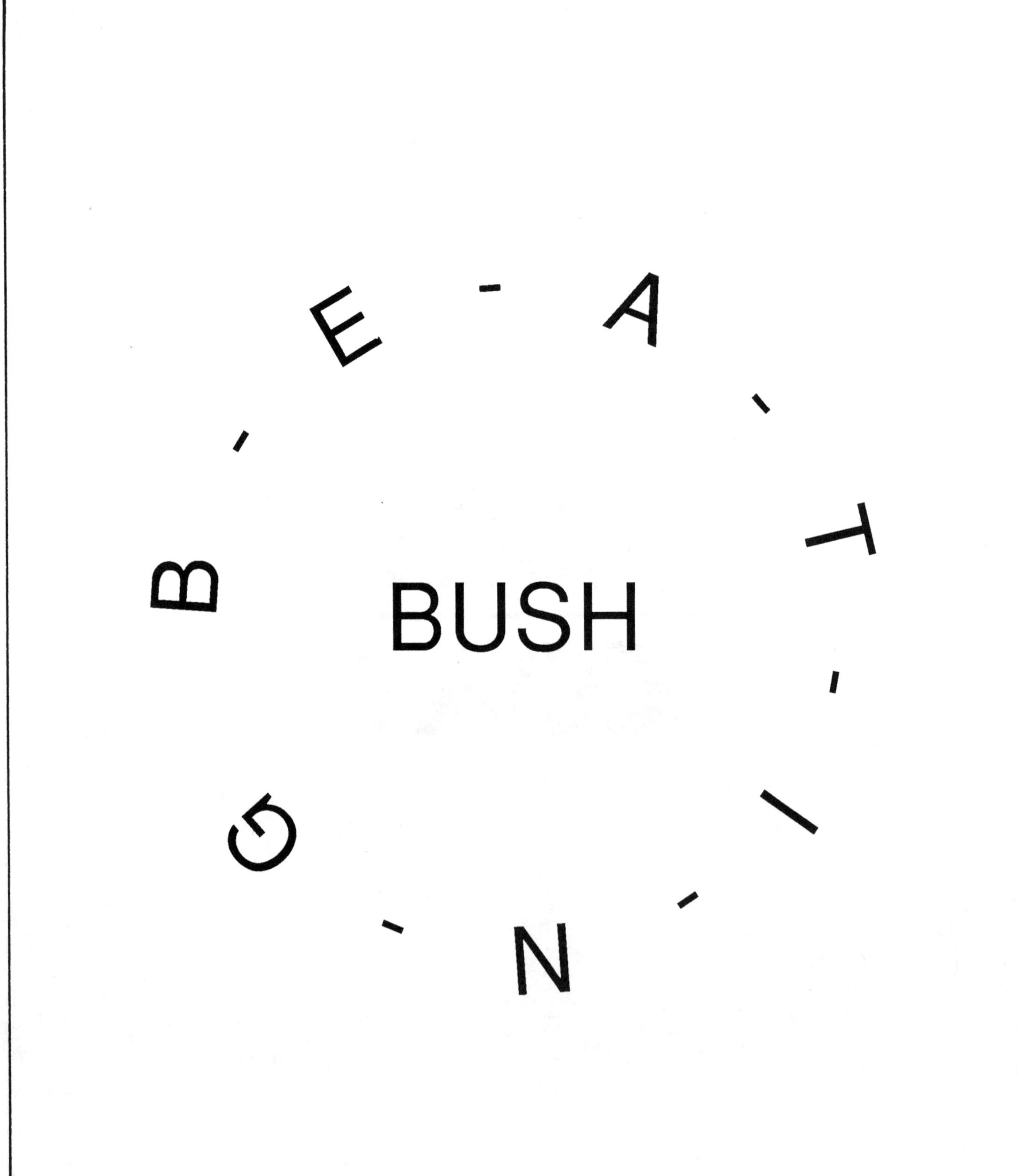

THINK-A-GRAM B1

POD
PP

HANDS
ACTIVITIES

THINK-A-GRAM B1

THINK-A-GRAM B1

CLASS MAIL

~~CLASS~~

~~CLASS~~

THINK-A-GRAM B1

THINK-A-GRAM B1

THINK-A-GRAM B1

THINK-A-GRAM B1

THINK-A-GRAM B1

T
O
E
A
R
T
H

THINK-A-GRAM B1

S
B
A
R
G
R
O
F

THINK-A-GRAM B1

KNEE
SIGN

THINK-A-GRAM B1

VATRYIN

DISCUSSION TOPIC

THINK-A-GRAM B1

FALUTIN

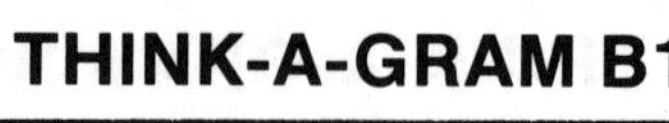
THINK-A-GRAM B1

DEEF

THINK-A-GRAM B1

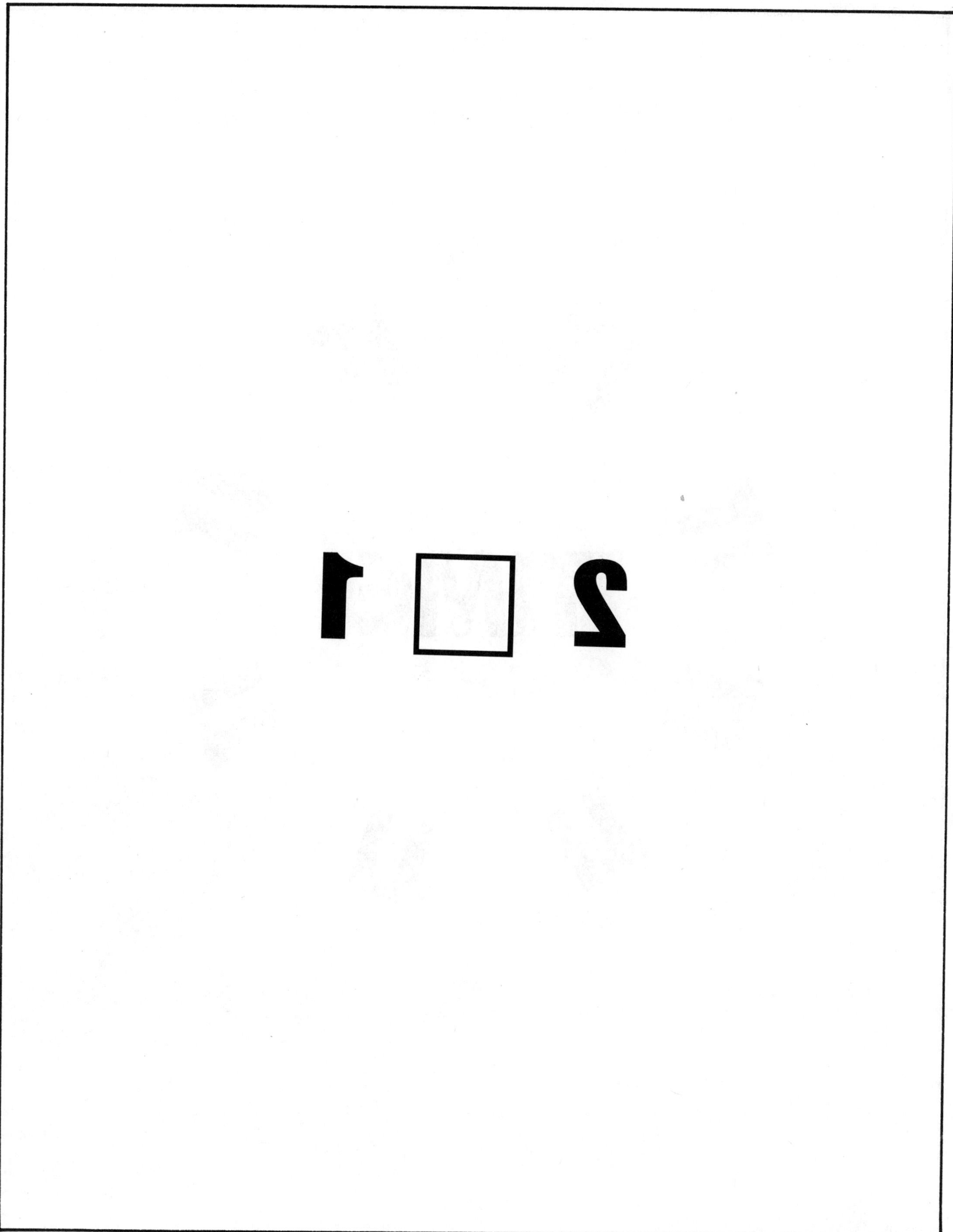

THINK-A-GRAM B1

FUNNY FUNNY
WORDS WORDS
WORDS WORDS

THINK-A-GRAM B1

G
N
I
K
C
A
R
C

THINK-A-GRAM B1

THINK-A-GRAM B1

GNIKLAT

TIME
MY HANDS

THINK-A-GRAM B1

LENTRUTHDING

SCORE
SCORE
SCORE
SCORE
7

THINK-A-GRAM B1

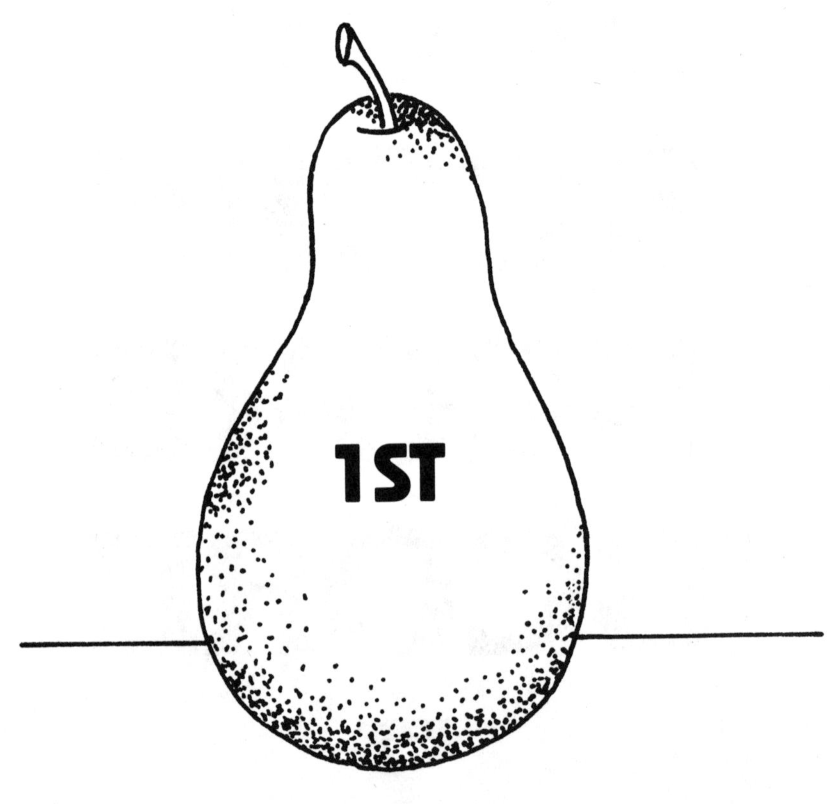

THINK-A-GRAM B1

WAY

PASS

THINK-A-GRAM B1

THINK-A-GRAM B1

ATTE N TION

THINK-A-GRAM B1

CLOUD CLOUD

CLOUD CLOUD

CLOUD CLOUD

CLOUD CLOUD

WALKING
CLOUD

THINK-A-GRAM B1

GIRLS CHASING

YELLOW
PAGES
walking

DRESSED
KILL
KILL

IN

MY HEAD

WINDER

NA
NA
FISH

THINK-A-GRAM B1

PLAY
WORDS

THINK-A-GRAM B1

NATION
WAR
NATION

THINK-A-GRAM B1

WORKED

TIME

THINK-A-GRAM B1

R
E
A
L

L
O
W

THINK-A-GRAM B1

THINK-A-GRAM B1

DOLLAR

THINK-A-GRAM B1

LEARN ROTE

THINK-A-GRAM B1

PLAPOWERCES

THINK-A-GRAM B1

THINK-A-GRAM B1

O_ER_T_O_

THINK-A-GRAM B1

SAILING
CCCCCCC

THINK-A-GRAM B1

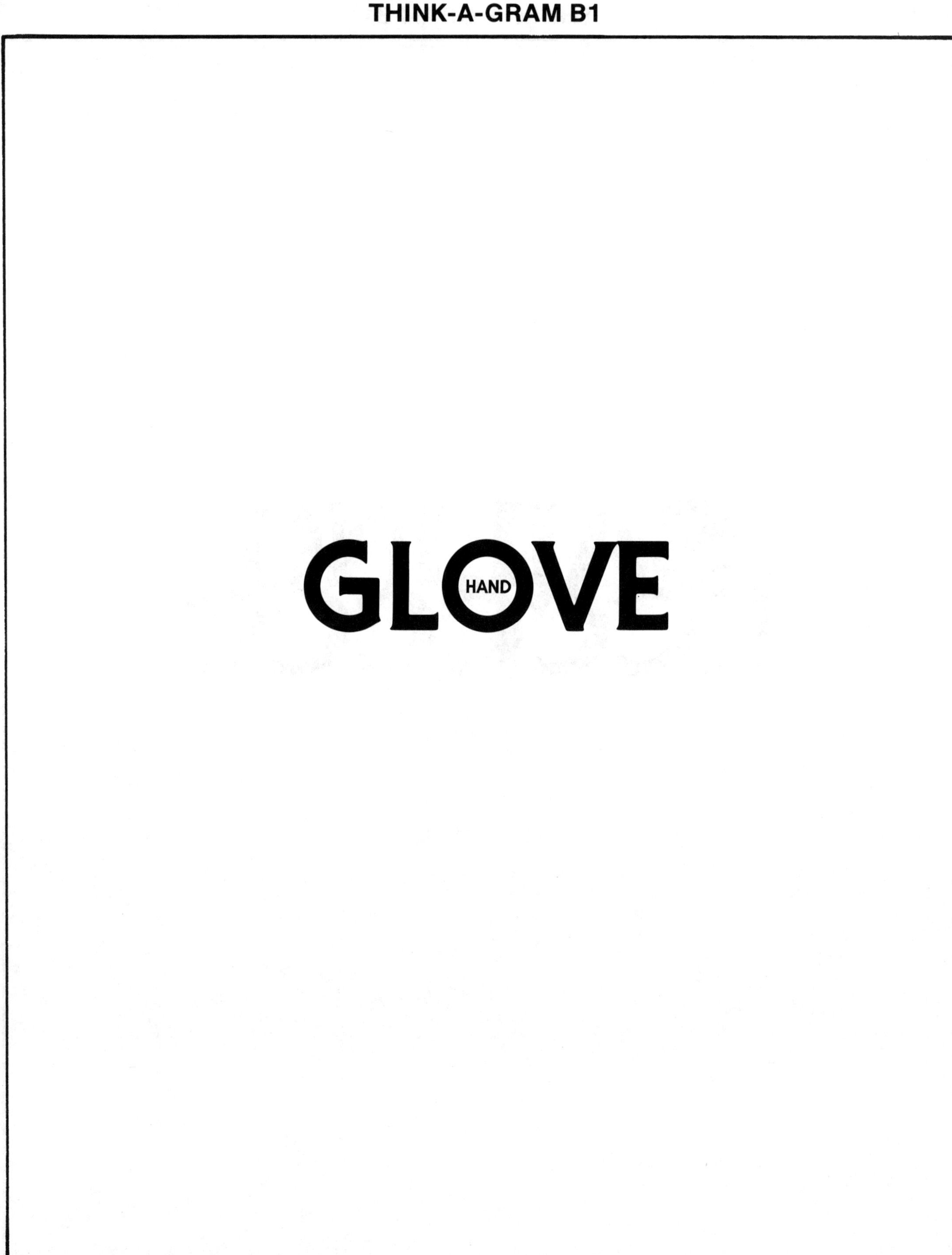

THINK-A-GRAM B1

WATER

SWIM

THINK-A-GRAM B1

SUNDAY
___
ALLS

THINK-A-GRAM B1

JOB
AN

THINK-A-GRAM B1

THINK-A-GRAM B1

TAKER
___
FRIENDLY

THINK-A-GRAM B1

GENE

THINK-A-GRAM B1

CAR
HAULED

THINK-A-GRAM B1

THINK-A-GRAM B1

THINK-A-GRAM B1

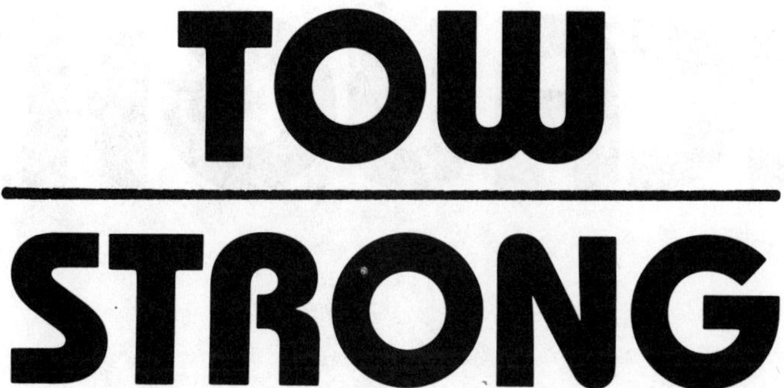

THINK-A-GRAM B1

THINK-A-GRAM B1

THINK-A-GRAM B1

COMFRIDEORT

THINK-A-GRAM B1

G
E
T
DAY
T
I
N
G

THINK-A-GRAM B1

DOWN
HIS LUCK

THINK-A-GRAM B1

BROOD

MISTAKES

THINK-A-GRAM B1

E
DESVPAIR
I
G

THINK-A-GRAM B1

R

E

L

L

I

F

THINK-A-GRAM B1

THINK-A-GRAM B1

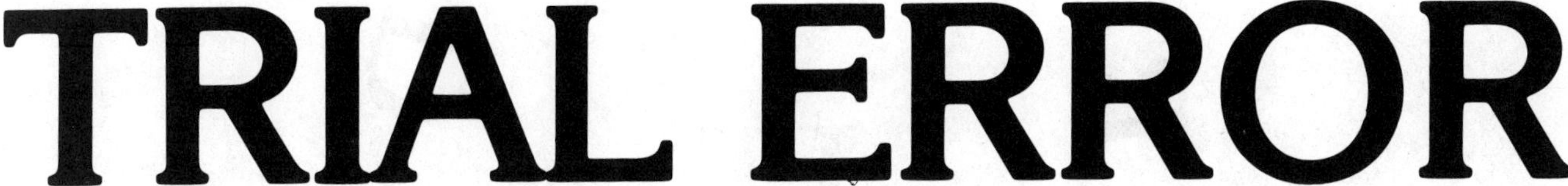

THINK-A-GRAM B1

THINK-A-GRAM B1

V

I

G

I

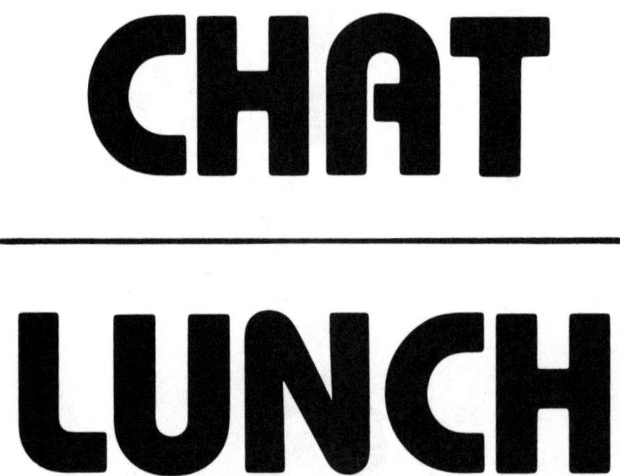
CHAT
LUNCH

INFORMATION

~~ALIGNMENT~~

ALIGNMENT